The Basho Poems

The Basho Poems
Keith Harrison

NODIN PRESS
Minneapolis, Minnesota

Some of these poems have appeared in the following places:
   The Carleton Miscellany
   25 Minnesota Poets (The Nodin Press)

Some of them were broadcast on several programs of the Australian Broadcasting Commission in Melbourne and Sydney, 1975 and 1976.

A shortened version of this book was printed in a limited, hand-printed edition by the Cyathus Press, Iowa City, 1975.

My thanks are due to the relevant editors and producers for permission to reprint them here.

   *

Copyright © 1981 Keith Harrison. All rights reserved. No part of this book may be produced in any form without the permission of Nodin Press, except for review purposes.

ISBN 0-931714-09-5

Nodin Press, a division of Micawber's Inc, 519 North Third Street, Minneapolis, Minnesota 55401.

Printed in U.S.A. at McNaughton and Gunn Inc., Ann Arbor, Michigan.

Book design and lettering by Elizabeth Edwards.

*For Arthur Gropen,
and for the taxi-driver in Washington, D.C.
who set me laughing*

Other Books by Keith Harrison

Points in a Journey, 1967 (Macmillan, London, and Dufour).

Two Variations on a Ground, 1967 (Turret Books).

Songs from the Drifting House, 1972 (Macmillan, London).

The Basho Poems, 1975 (Cyathus Press, Iowa City: limited edition).

Without Boundaries, 1979 (Francité, Montreal). Translations from the French of H. A. Bouraoui.

A Town and Country Suite, 1980 (Sternum Press, Minneapolis).

In preparation:

Keepers of the Orchard (new poems)

The Sense of Falling

Time of the Goat (a prose narrative)

At the Marriage of Peleus and Thetis: a New Translation of *Catullus #64* (with Linda Clader)

Sir Gawain and the Green Knight (a new translation)

Contents

Basho Beside the Mountain	1
The Thing Direct	7
Reply to the Grammarians 8	
Hangover Poem 9	
Quick Shadow 10	
Sketch for an Aesthetic 11	
He Recapitulates/Forecasts the Stages of His Life 12	
His Transmigrations	15
Traveling Toward the Vache Qui Pue *River* 16	
Basho Rejects Hinduism or Marshall McLuhan in India 17	
Basho's Marginal Songs 18	
Railroad Tanka 20	
Minnesota Winterdrive 21	
Basho in Melbourne 22	
Seven Dream Poems	23
Basho Devises His Obituaries	29
An Interview with Basho	35
A Sentimental Elegy 44	
From Basho's Poems on the Moods and Modes of the Pigeon	45
Notes on the Basho Poems	69

Basho Beside the Mountain

Basho Beside the Mountain

There was this message
from K'en Lee's nephew to his father's brother —
or was it to his father's brother's wife?
Walking beside the mountain,
it occurred to him that he was very small
and somewhat stupid.
    *

The mountain watched him as he moved:
slow dot around the giant base.
    *

A cormorant pierced the smooth
silk-sheen of water under the mountain.
Basho held his breath, went down with him
down and down, hunting.
His head began to pound. Red-faced
he suddenly blew it all out.

It's clear I could never be a cormorant, he said.
    *

Basho flopped down
on a rustic bridge. There were a few
fat carp dodging among the weeds.
K'en Lee's nephew came by.

*Why are you looking down with such intensity —
do you seek Enlightenment in water?*

Neck's tired, Basho said —
been looking too long
at that bloody mountain.

    *

When the harlot confronted Basho
her jasmine smell almost undid him.
As they undressed he was amazed
at the loveliness of her flanks, the way
her small breasts bobbled when she laughed.
There are two kinds of harlot, Basho said.
*For the first I have the images of
spring water pelting over rocks,
a gazelle, a pitcher brimming with honey.*

And for the second?

I find it difficult to think about such people, Basho said.

Then he pinned her to the mountain.
All afternoon.

Afterward it was very simple.

There was the mountain over them, and under them.
There was the bellsound winding over the lake.
And there was jasmine.

    *

At about the fortieth twist
in the mountain road
a drunken bandit came at him.
Empty your pockets, he said.

I'm a poet, Basho said.
I live off other people's money.

The bandit lunged at him.

Basho kicked him in the cods. Stalked on.

    *

Very well, I'll tell you the Thousand Things, said Basho.

There's bird's wing, the smell of it,
there's the grain of rice that eats you,
jasmine petals on the executioner's sleeve.
There's knock of water against the keel, the drum
   at the center.

Certain wines whose bouquets drift into eternity.

There's also rock which is what it is,
the uncommitted bandit who is what he is not
there are dragons that seem mountains
and mountains that seem dragons

and finally, there's the mountain.

That's not a thousand!

Damn right it is, said Basho. Count them again.

    *

Basho's wife said:
                Where have you been all day?

Pinning a harlot to the mountain.

You, bag of bones? Your head's so full of dreams you couldn't tell a woman from a turkey.

Perhaps it was the jasmine, Basho said.

But his wife, stirring a pot, didn't hear him.

    *

After his descent from the mountain
Basho wrote three poems.
The poems were:

(1) A wind-blasted gull
    grips the
    crow's nest:
    the pine bends as the earth
    hog-rolls.

(2) Moonlight
    floods my window:
    if a friend looks in tonight
    he'll darken me.

(3) Unbroken light on the lake.
    The cormorant's hunting.
    Heavens, four hours!

Basho read these poems to his wife.

> *Nothing important
> can be done
> in seventeen
> syllables*, she said.

The Thing Direct

Reply to the Grammarians

I am a knockabout man of little learning
and almost nothing that will pass for tact.
I like the thing direct: the wolf's wet fang,
howl of a new-born pig. Appetite. Fact.
The soft *plup* of plum-falls in October
's my kind of music either drunk or sober.
Against the tune that your grammarians sing
I set the landscape of the pigeon's wing.
You who stand back and crookedly explain
can never quell this hunger in my brain.

Hangover Poem

Must've been the sākĕ
immature and sour, that
we drank together:
the mind beneath my hat
flicks about like a feather,
but cannot find its bird.

Quick Shadow

Strolling in the garden
comes to spires of lettuce, tall as himself.
A pear-tree snapped by the wind
sags over the ruined cabbages.
He looks up.
A shadow moves across the mountain
very quickly.

He shivers,
trundles his clanking bones indoors.

Sketch for an Aesthetic

If a man is intent on writing,
Basho remarked to a stupid cousin,
he has to study details:
color of a tiger's belch, the way
wind wobbles
before it polishes the pomegranates,
the shape of adverbs in sultry weather;
you also have to understand
the irrationality of water,
how it behaves when you kick it.

When you come to the end of all that
you have to study Man,
the creature whose defining virtue's
to bite the same behind that he tries to sit on.

He Recapitulates/Forecasts the Stages of His Life

Three Minutes Before Birth
Someone poured cold water on my toe.
Insulted, I drew it back, decided
to stay inside.

At Three
A fat fish stood up
suddenly out of the pool
and flapped himself
into the sun.

At Fourteen
I begin to understand calligraphy.
From this moment I will be lost.

At Twenty
Blasted with love's excess
I plunge down the mountain
and break my ankle in a ditch.

At Thirty
Whatever engine is running me, it
missed a stroke. There, on the
wet roadway, as I looked at the clouds bunched up,
the blank water.

At Forty
If the evil persists at this time
good may never be at hand.

At Fifty
"Lotus blossoms on smooth water . . ."

At Sixty
"Smooth water . . ."

At Seventy
Lubricious fantasies. The last
twitch, the first
twitch.

His Transmigrations

Traveling Toward the *Vache Qui Pue* River
or
Basho Attempts to Translate Robert Bly

I am walking very slowly across Minnesota
inside a car with no engine and no seats.
I have left the seats in a hundred country towns and the old
squat around on them and dream of onions. In country towns
sitting down is never the same as standing.
It is dusk but I have forgotten why.
It is also Minnesota, whatever that means.

The moon floats out of the turkey sheds
dragging the turkeys and their smells with it.
The soybeans are myopic, you can hear them
sulking and kicking each others' shins.
The lamplight collapses on the grass
like a spavined frog.

Suddenly the moon flaps past
and smashes itself against the box-elder.
Wearing my bottomless car I slouch over a bridge
and listen with unspeakable sympathy
while two Aquarians try to screw their boat to the river.
I teach them a chorus of the Vache Qui Pue, and they
uncrew the boat. They have never heard
of Missoula, Montana, where I was happy.

Basho Rejects Hinduism
or
Marshall McLuhan in India

tat tvam asi

tas tati mav

masa tat vit

ma's a tit vat

's i'm a tat vat

(a titva tat, 'm?)

vatsit mata

ta ma, vat's it!

"*tat tvam asi*" = TAT AM I.

              VAST

              AS T.V.

Basho's Marginal Songs

Happy Day Among the Elephant People
Father, blubber, grease body
tumbling through the sky.

    "The earth is very peculiar."

The Sage Who Came by While Basho Was Trying to Restore His Rotten Pear-Tree
I met a man who lived too long;
this was the burden of his song,
frog's breath, bird-lime, blow on your twisted nail.

I met a man who lived too slow
seventy years as these things go
his eye turned in and his tooth yellow.

Both long and slow died in a fog
(two withered tails who'd lost their dog)
one frozen hard beside a log —
one falling far, very rapidly

He Rebukes His Underwear
Fortnightly.
Fought nightly.

Late Breakfast
Bean curd
bean herd
been heard
been turd
been had
absurd
merd

The Crocodiles Who Stayed Too Long
Whatever the fig meant
was no figment

Whatever the pig lent
was no pigment payment

Whatever the horses say
there was no horseplay

There were only the spaces, where they'd thrashed about.
The ashes, the bleeding petals, the debris.

Railroad Tanka

I walk the gleaming rails
ahead of me
two feet
above the black horizon
the full moon thunders toward me.

Minnesota Winterdrive

I said to them that this was all the time hardly even moving you have this huge back of the beast I said a million miles in any direction are all the same with the road winding through our eyes and out the back of our heads always I said this is always and no way out of it road road road and any direction of snow snow west and snow snow east where if any god has a hot body he doesn't put his bum down here I said the sun goes five months inside and it stays inside like a cinnamon bear in a hole I said they said why don't you give over you go on too much I said this is a road road oh yes this is a road and what you think you can do about it with all the driving it all just stays the same big fat blackwhite beast like the backside of Betelgeuse all ahead of us and all around and the cold sun crouching in his hole I said they said Jesus belt up get him out of here I said laughing like hell I said you can't even stop this is the road road this is the road.

Basho in Melbourne

I walk through the long
suburbs questioning.

No one replies.

Seven Dream Poems

Seven Dream Poems

1

I am in bed with a harlot. We are both covered in sprays of jasmine. There are so many flowers that I cannot find the harlot. An eagle, balanced on the bed-stead points a red beak down at us. I leap up and strangle it and hurl its hot body down into the market place. When I turn round the harlot has gone, though on the heaped flowers she has left a discreet white card. I turn the card over. It is blank on both sides. I stand there shivering, covered with eagle feathers.

2

This time I am inside a jasmine flower. A procession of dead people go by, carrying bootlaces in their right hand. In the other hand they hold flags inscribed with an indecipherable message. They begin to whirl the bootlaces rapidly. They make a noise like a thousand bull-roarers. A dead arm cracks off like a limb from a plaster doll and crashes into the foliage beneath my hideout. I crawl deeper into the flower.

3

The bowl of a brilliantly lacquered lute presses into my belly and begins humming as the wind drives through it. I tune it with my toes. Aha, it sings like a turtle! I rub a leg experimentally across the strings. At first nothing happens, then the hairs get caught and it hurts like hell. I wake my wife up with the shouting.

4

I am rowing a huge black bull across the lake. The bull snuffs the air and wheels forward like a dolphin. I throw back my head, warrior-style and shout *Grah, Grah* into the waves. A storm beats up and we barrel through the black waves singing together. Suddenly there is a haven of sunlight and calm water. My wife has laid out the breakfast in a little bay. There are plates of wild honey and sherbet and a tiny salad of frogs' legs doused in wine. All the plates are floating on lotus leaves. The bull noses among them delicately. Kingfishers flash emerald and scarlet, then dissolve in air. Astride the bull I eat with aristocratic nonchalance. My wife prepares more dishes on the shore.

5

A line of soldiers plunges down the mountain, beating drums, dislodging stones. They break down my door and ram me against the wall.

— Where are all your filthy poems? the leader asks.
— Over there, in that bowl of moonlight.

They smash the bowl and hand the poems round. The soldiers eat them. When they've finished the leader leaps at me and yells into my face WE WANT MORE.

— There aren't any more, you evil-smelling bastard.

I try to kick him but my boot turns into a swan.

6

I write a perfect poem which gathers itself together and walks off the page with a light sneeze. It goes outdoors and squats under the pear-tree. I can hear it talking to the lettuce.

7

A chess-board. Myself against my brother. The kings are taken and only two pieces are left on the board — both white, both pawns. They are on the same file, with one square between them. We shout obscenities about who should move. My wife rushes in and angrily sets the pieces alongside each other. We take each other "en passant." Then we re-arrange the board. Each player now has half the black and half the white pieces. What delicious complications! We play on serenely.

Basho Devises His Obituaries

Basho Devises His Obituaries

1

The poet Basho is dead. A light has gone out, a gloom has settled on the land. From hundreds of miles the mourners troop toward his tomb, his verses resounding in their hearts. One man, crazed with sorrow, walked off the road and, losing his way in a marsh, drowned himself. There is no end to the sorrow. The governor has sent out functionaries to keep the farmers at their work. But still they leave the fields.

The career and person of Basho are swaddled in enigma. Even those who thought they knew him well find him elusive. On the face of it his life was exemplary. He kept a garden. By habit he rose early, sharpened his pencils and wrote till noon. In the afternoon, fatigued by the labour of composition, he slept. His life was of a simplicity that flowed in everything he touched. Apart from a single indiscretion on the mountain he was faithful, diligent, clear-headed, robust, manly, majestic in purpose, forbidding in repose — and without question he was the best poet in the largest village of the region.

Basho was the ghost in all of you. In a world of complex sewers he asserted the radical normality of trees and pigeons. He understood the quality of metals and the delicate grain of amethyst and agate. The unctuous plumage of the crow, the taste of wild berries, the flesh of women were a language to him. He spent his life trying to translate that language and, once or twice, succeeded. Misunderstood in his life, he now begins his long dialogue with creatures underground. If he can persuade them, maybe they will lift him out so that, once again, he can plunge his head into a spray of blossoms and run his words like fingers through the warm fur of the world.

2

When Basho awoke in his bed
and found he was bloody near dead
he cried out in wonder
"I've made a huge blunder —
I had such a good line in my head."

He took up his pen in a flash
and slumped at his desk with a crash
when a harlot appeared
and seductively leered.
Her visit quite settled his hash.

3

I knew him quite well in his younger days. Frankly, I thought he was a mean little sod. Stuck-up. Enormous opinion of himself. He hated what our group was doing because most of us were writing better than he was. I liked some of the early things, but after forty he started to write reams of inane pap and all that stuff about pigeons and jasmine. God, who needs it? My own theory is that he was an old lecher posing as a poet — you know, the grave look toward the distant mountains, the sigh of impatience at a question which he thought beneath him. Most of the time he was just too dense to understand.

Most of all he was cruel and ruthless. Do you know that one time up on the mountain he just lashed out and kicked an old farmer in the groin? And then he went around spreading this story about how he was attacked by a bandit. My God, no self-respecting bandit would go near Basho. You could see straightaway that he was penniless. And he'd been wearing the same robe for about forty years, and it stank.

4

All my life I have been afraid of death. I persuaded myself that the thought of death was boring — the hand hesitating over the page, a vision of rats and skulls. Such things keep a man from his business, I thought. To make a small thing well a man needs joy. And who can be joyful when his head is full of death?

And yet, at last, this place is most amusing. They have been eating me for days, and as they eat they carry away the fear. I am becoming part of a vast empire of leaves and minerals. It is a kind of opulent dozing, and I find to my surprise that I am irreducible. Occasionally I hear the sound of people above me, mourning, and one day an old gaffer fell into a marsh, crying out my name. Most amusing. I'll try to reach him.

5

Basho is dead and his ideas.
What can a woman make of that?
Burn his clothes, cover his ears.
Carve on his tomb of modest slate
He was my husband. Fifty years.

An Interview with Basho

An Interview with Basho

Basho: "The eye by way of the field-mouse to the comma; the tooth by way of the hiccup to the dream . . ."

Interviewer: *What was that?*

B: Nothing. Let's move under the damson tree. It catches the light beautifully about this time. Look at the way the fishboat pushes its arrowhead slowly across the lake. And if you listen carefully you can hear the creak of its rowlocks.

Int: *When did you first start writing?*

B: It's like the pain in your back. It's hard to tell when it got there.

Int: *Can you remember what prompted you to begin?*

B: Pigeons.

Int: *Pigeons?*

B: And cormorants. I've always envied cormorants. Though eating raw fish is hardly my idea of a decent meal. Imagine that frantic wriggling in your throat. Ugh!

Int: *What was it about the pigeons?*

B: The way they flap round like old rags. The angles they make in the wind. There's nothing very beautiful about them. Piglets of the air I call them. But I like the way they launch themselves like a suicide from a ledge then, just when you think they're going to fall to pieces, they suddenly fly.

Int: *What does all that have to do with poetry though?*

B: One line for an image, one image to the line.

Int: *What does that mean?*

B: I'm not sure. I'm working at it.

Int: *Let's go back to the pigeons.*

B: Very well. I'm back.

Int: *I still don't understand.*

B: What don't you understand?

Int: *How they got you started. Pigeons and poetry. I don't get it.*

B: In one language I can think of there are over fifty words for the notion of "to tremble." — all of them carrying a slight but distinct nuance. Our language is lazy; we have only three or four. Which means that when we come to the flight of the pigeon we are almost completely inarticulate. Yet you can count at least 81 characteristic movements — counterturn, bank, the wing-tip stand and the side-slip — all kinds of movements. The thing is to find a verb for them and the emotions they awaken. The whole language a kind of verb.

Int: *Have you been exclusively concerned with pigeons all your life?*

B: Heavens, no! That was only a start. Lately I have been studying the rhythm of sea-weed, the texture of black bulls. Lots of things.

Int: *Does the study of linguistics help a writer?*

B: Linguistics talks of phonemes. My basic unit is the croneme.

Int: *The croneme? What kind of a thing is that?*

B: A croneme is the unit of concentration, resonance, opulence and nonsense.

Int: *Can you give an example?*

B: Any word in a good poem is a croneme. One of our modern masters has a narrative which at one point contains the amazing sentence: *So*. In that word he captures very accurately one moment of the pigeon's flight — a tragic moment as it happens: a young boy has just lost his hand and the poet writes, *So*. Very curious. A damned cheek, really.

Int: *But* So *is a phoneme, isn't it?*

B: Maybe. But it's a croneme as well.

Int: *I'm afraid you've lost me.*

B: Don't worry, this is difficult stuff. Break yourself off a plum. They're quite delicious.

Int: *No thanks. Bad digestion. I have to live exclusively off bean curds.*

B: Bean curds! Poor man — even the look of bean curds . . . Well, never mind, let's get on . . .

Int: *Do you think that this is a bad century for a writer to live in?*

B: It certainly is. All centuries are bad. A few years ago in the South someone unearthed a tablet about three thousand years old. On it was an inscription from a father to a son which read, "Take care son, things are going to hell. The end of civilization is near." There have always been gloomy people. We need them for comic relief.

Trouble is that gloominess is nowadays a social obligation. Ask a teacher how his students are doing. "Idiots," he replies. "I work myself sick trying to get the simplest things into them . . . the young are falling apart . . ." And everybody says Yes, yes, it's awful isn't it? Or you go down to the fish market and ask about the catch and the fishmonger says "Almost nothing, the lake's fished out. We're going to starve . . ." And he nods his head and his fat cheeks wobble. It's a kind of convention.

Int: *Do you think the schools are to blame?*

B: Perhaps. But schools have always been bad as well. It's unrealistic to expect them to be otherwise. Mediocre and safe views are the staple of schools. There's been no essential change in that for thousands of years. But there is a difference nowadays. Stupidity used to be accepted as one of the hazards. Now we celebrate it — enthrone it, even. There's such an accumulation of printed rubbish and such an efficient bureaucracy that we can't get out from under it. It's become *de rigueur* to be gloomy and stupid.

Int: *What about the teaching of poetry?*

B: Universal literacy has bred a generation of deaf-mutes. They can *see* all right. But the other senses are asleep. So the whole question of the meaning of a poem has been reduced to one dimension:

> Along the rough rock, an ant
> > staggers under his load:
> He's brought the beetle low, but the
> > huge wing pins him down.

To read that correctly you have to get the accents right. Otherwise you make nonsense of it.

Int: *But you yourself spoke of nonsense as the fourth characteristic of your croneme — now it seems you're reviling it . . .*

B: Ho, you've pinned me! But watch out, I shall shake you off! The croneme itself is nonsense. I just made it up while we were talking.

Int: *You mean I shouldn't believe in it?*

B: Oh no, you *should* believe in it — it's very serious. There are two kinds of nonsense — the nonsense of poetry and the nonsense of nonsense. "The lamplight falls on all fours on the grass . . ." is probably the first kind — though that's a problematical example, I admit. And if I gave you the 81 poems on the flight of the pigeon you'd have a hell of a time deciding which is which. I did, I can assure you.

Int: *You mean you've written them? I've never seen a copy. Where are they?*

B: I burned them. And the pigeons go on flying.

Int: *How does one tell nonsense from nonsense?*

B: A marvellous question to end with — and look, my wife is bringing us tea. Lacking a harlot there's nothing like jasmine tea, don't you think? And by the way, I should have added a fifth notion to the croneme.

Int: *What's that?*

B: Luck. But there's nowhere to put it. Croneme-*l?* What kind of a word would that make? Let's move out into the sun. Ah, look at that — the steam from our teacups is dissolving the mountain!

A Sentimental Elegy

I wish at least that I could die tonight:
nothing goes right,
all goes right.

I know the central trope reads "born to die."
Pains in my chest
and the crib
rocking.

Flies bang their
silly heads.

Who will conciliate?
And what to reconcile?

Sad, yet tipped with humour,
the moments edge over
the moments edge
the moments
the
the

From Basho's Poems
on the Moods and Modes
of the Pigeon

```
                              l
                          f
                                    y          n
                    g         n                        g
                       o           s        i
                    e
             p    i
```

                    into

                              up
                      breaks

                  barn window
                        through the empty
            smoke pours
        a stream of whirring

Dog yaps

These days of wind
I am no better
than a snapped umbrella

*stay low, fatty, you're coming
unglued*

Bugged by the landlords,
the hard-beaked sparrows,
we take our stand
behind the shit-banks on
the Bank of England.

rou-cou-ler
a thousand times
the sound goes round
the barn
rou-cou
rou-cou
rou-cou   rou-ler
soon our language will be found
meanwhile
these idiot syllables
will have to do
will do   will do

They're packing horse-dung in a pile.
The horses cannot understand it.

Your tires
kick out pebbles,
my bomb-body
waddles across your
raked gravel.
You say I'm common
as burdock, crabweed —

but when this barn's
burned and eaten
around your absence
our wings will make
rough music.

We bubble like pools of porridge.
Hyde Park Corner.
We've heard it all:

Politics. The art of the
crunchable.

Ice in our wings:
our metal bodies

utterly still

the moon
wheeling slowly
around the empty farm

A white cat crunching wing-bones
eyes me from the granary floor.
Look to your onions, arrogant bum:
lost in your greedy delirium
with pigeon-lice pricking your skin
you're only a bundle of burning fur —
a complex meal that eats itself,
an ecological sewer.

Dear Cat: I'm heading South.
I've my own lice to lead.

P.S. Die. Immediately.

All the ladies are fat again,
and some so pleased with themselves
they bounce their eggs down

                                                        thirty feet.

A sound as real
and round as a pebble,
a big song bouncing off the moon
the rise, the roll, the carol, the creation:
that kind of thing.

Nothing except this dry click in my throat.

They've blocked us out of the barn
with chicken wire and chunks of wood.

Above us the vast October sky.

O the beasts of the earth have their lairs
and the Son of Man has overstuffed chairs
and a wide sweet-smelling bed —
but this night
under the horrible, thin starlight
the Son of Pigeon
has nowhere to lay his head.

A startled pigeon
jumped into my eye, and snapped
the lid.

(sings)
IF I HAD THE WINGS OF A SWALLOW . . .

That way, madness.

Comes a moment in the affairs of Pigeon
when almost everything seems dung.
The reason for the vision's plain:
almost everything here *is* dung.

Saturday: a blue sound
full of pigeons

I have been thinking about dogs.
No dog thinks of me.
In this respect I am wasting my life.

Here's Basho again.
Mooching about in his dirty robe.
What a bore . . .
Fancies he's inventing us
with all those words.
Hey Basho, take that!

It rhymes.

Hard to think
with this idiot moonlight
pouring down:
horses in the yard
can't shake their shadows,
warm engines running,
engines and insects
throbbing under the moon.

Each thing fastened to its shadow.

Most of the statements
my feathers make
stop short.

Like that.

Notes on the Basho Poems

Not only the plan but a good deal of the original imagery was suggested by a student whose haiku lacked a syllable. This book is the missing syllable.

*

The Penguin edition of Basho's diaries, which I have not read, has a number of pages missing.

*

There has been some speculation about the identity of Basho. Some have claimed that he is the re-incarnation of the ancient Japanese poet who is at present living near Dreck, Missouri — which, of course, is nonsense.

*

Basho is a fictional character but his wife is real.

Hackberry Hollow
Northfield, Minnesota
1975 & 1980

Australian poet Keith Harrison, during the course of a slow journey around the world, was delayed by a snowstorm in Southern Minnesota, where he has remained for 13 years sending out muffled messages to the world, of which this book is one. Others are on the way, including a new collection of occidental poems called *Keepers of the Orchard*, as well as a number of translations, and a short prose narrative, *Time of the Goat*.